EASYGROWTH PUBLISHING'S

WORKBOOK

FOR

LIMITLESS

BY

JIM KWIK

Upgrade Your Brain, Learn Anything Faster and Unlock your Exceptional Life

WORKBOOK & SUMMARY

TABLE OF CONTENTS

Note to Readers

This is an unofficial workbook for Jim Kwik's Limitless: Upgrade your Brain, Learn Anything Faster and Unlock your Exceptional Life designed to enrich your experience of the original book, and give you practical steps to apply the author's message to your life. Buy the Original book by scanning the QR code below.

PART I

FREE YOUR MIND

We Already Carry the Magic Needed to Transform the World Within Us.

CHAPTER ONE
BECOMING LIMITLESS

Jim Kwik narrates his path to becoming limitless to realizing his brain's enormous power and amazing capabilities.

Jim was not always the sought after brain coach he is today. In fact, to imagine he would be a brain coach back when he was a child would have been the wildest of impossible dreams. While he was young, an accident rendered him learning-deficient, and at one time, he became known as "the boy with the broken brain."

It was not until he visited his friend's family about giving up on college that he got a life-changing encounter.

His friend's dad asked him how school was going.

That innocent question was the key that opened up the floodgates of emotions that had already built within Jim Kwik.

He broke down and cried so hard.

Jim explained his "broken brain" status to his friend's dad.

And what was the reply?

His friend's dad asked him three questions that you have to answer here too.

"**Why** are you in school? (Or why are you doing what's featuring most prominently in your life now? It could be your job, a project, or a relationship). What do you want to **be**? What do you want to **have**?"

Answering these questions will help you tap into your drive and purpose, which is necessary to become limitless (to be discussed later).

_____

_____

_____

_____

_____

_____

_____

_____

_____

_____

_____

_____

_____

_____

_____

_____

_____

_____

_____

_____

_____

When Jim had finished answering the questions by writing a bucket list, his friend's dad gave him some books and asked him to read one title a week.

Trying to read the books his friend's father gave him coupled with his academic books, Jim passed one day and fell down the stairs, sustaining yet another head injury. It was at the hospital that Jim reconsidered his stance and began to think...

What if he didn't just work hard but taught himself a better way to learn? Was there not a better way to remain focused and assimilate the information he tried to learn? What if there is a faster, more efficient and effective way to learn? So began Kwik's obsession with the art of learning.

He kept aside his academic books and studied books on learning theory, neuroscience and personal growth. After a couple of months, Jim discovered he was actually better at learning, and he could now train his focus. This knowledge brought forth a new feeling of confidence that Jim didn't quite have before, and since he now knew what to do going forward, the "boy with the broken brain" slowly became a genius who is now a sought after brain fitness expert.

If knowledge is power, learning is our superpower; we must learn how to access this superpower.

The ability to be limitless resides in you, ready to be tapped. But there are perceived restrictions that you must overcome to become limitless.

Jim believed for so long that he was the boy with the broken brain, and there was nothing he could do. The change came when he realized that his perceived restrictions were no restrictions; they were just hurdles he had to overcome to become limitless.

What are the challenges you struggle with every day? What do you think is limiting you from achieving your desired results? Is it your inability to comprehend what you read? Is it the fact that you forget faster than you read? The perceived limitations may be about any aspect of your life. Write those down.

_____

_____

_____

_____

_____

_____

_____

Being limitless is not only but speed reading, remembering more, and staying focused. Yes, it is all that, but more. It is about progressing beyond what you currently believe possible. It is about unlimiting the limitations you just wrote down in the last exercise.

But you must have a blueprint, key or model to becoming limitless, and Jim Kwik offers this. The key is the **Limitless 3Ms**.

- Limitless Mindset (The What)
- Limitless Motivation (The Why)
- Limitless Methods (The How)

If you are not already performing at your full potential, it is because there is a limit in the deeply held assumptions and beliefs you have about yourself (mindset), or a limit in your purpose and drive (motivation), or worse still, there is a limit in the process you use (the method).

Therefore, the book Limitless teaches how to cultivate limitless mindset, motivation, and methods.

What are the limitless 3Ms that are necessary to be limitless? Write them down and discuss what you understand about them.

_____

_____

_____

_____

_____

_____

_____

_____

_____

_____

_____

_____

_____

CHAPTER TWO

WHY THIS MATTERS NOW

It is all-important to get limitless in your academics, relationships, or job now more than ever. It is also necessary that you develop the superpowers that lie within you, waiting to be awakened. By superpowers, it is not necessarily meant the ability to throw webs from between your fingers, fly in iron suits or shoot lasers from your eyes. It is rather meant that you can develop superhuman abilities like laser focus, iron-clad memory, mindfulness, and superior mental attitude.

However, Jim Kwik postulates four super villains that you must hunt down before opening the path to becoming *limitless.*

And while technological advancement may not be bad in itself, these super-villains have grown from the use of advanced technology.

These digital villains are:

Digital Deluge

Thanks to robust technological advancement, information explosion gives us too much information to process and no time to handle this extreme volume of information. The amount of information we have to process greatly takes its toll on the quality of our lives.

This constant barrage of information has negative effects on your mental health.

If you never let your mind wander for a moment but always feed it with a barrage of information to process, the result becomes poor memory, mental fog and fatigue.

What does your schedule look like? Go over it and schedule 30 minutes of your day every day to spend away from technology, to clear your mind and relax.

DAY	ANTI-DELUGE TIME
Sunday	
Monday	
Tuesday	
Wednesday	
Thursday	
Friday	
Saturday	

Digital Distraction

We no longer leave our devices, they are always with us, and we are ever connected to them. Because of our ever-connected devices, we are now finding it difficult more than ever to forge meaningful connections with friends and acquaintances. We are hit with new texts, likes, and notifications from social media every moment of our being.

Most of us don't know how to manage the distractions we receive from our connected devices every day, so we try to multi-task everything in, feeding our distraction muscles and waning out our ability to concentrate.

Have you ever wanted to carry out and activity but decided to check a notification on your mobile phone, got buried in your devices and didn't carry out the activity again? Describe your experience. Does it frustrate you?

_____

_____

_____

_____

_____

_____

_____

_____

Digital Dementia

Neuroscientist Manfred Spitzer uses the term *Digital Dementia* to describe how information technology leads to the breakdown of cognitive abilities and long-term memory.

We no longer have to remember anyone's phone number, perform simple math calculations from memory, or memorize directions to a particular restaurant in a new city because our smartphones are always there to do the work for us.

But the research shows that our brains are like muscles that get strengthened each time we use them, but we are failing to use them. And just as there are physical consequences to using the elevator rather than the stairs, there are consequences for using smartphones for every day's cognitive tasks rather than our brains.

Digital Deduction

How do you feel when someone tries to impose their thinking on you?

_____

_____

_____

_____

_____

Sadly, we are slowly ceding our thinking faculties to our smartphones and the vast amount of available online information. We can now get answers to each question we ask and differing opinions and treatises on various topics at the click of a mouse.

The result is that deduction, a core component of critical thinking, is being replaced by the hundreds of opinions we can get about a specific topic online.

But why will you turn over this liberating power of critical thinking to a device?

So write down a decision you need to make. It may be connected to your job, school, family or anything at all. Then schedule out time to work on that decision without the help of any digital device.

_____

_____

_____

_____

_____

_____

_____

_____

Now that you are aware of the four villains, what do you think about them? Which of the villains fight you the most and constantly disrupts your productivity and peace of mind? Write it down and develop a strategy to combat it. It might be by spending less time on your smart phone or exercising your brain more regularly rather than using information technology all the time for solving everyday problems.

_____

_____

_____

_____

_____

_____

_____

_____

_____

_____

_____

CHAPTER THREE

YOUR LIMITLESS BRAIN

Right there, between your ears, is the most complex machine ever created. Your brain is *limitless,* and you can become that too if you tap into its enormous power. The human brain separates us from the rest of creation; humans can't fly, we don't have tremendous physical power, we are not the biggest, but we're the most dominant of all creatures because of highly advanced brains.

Your brain generates more than 70,000 thoughts per day and works at unimaginable speeds. It is just what it is, a hyper super-computer.

But if your brain is awesome, why are you still caught up in feelings of inadequacy? Why are overload, distraction, and forgetfulness, affecting you so much?

The answer is you have yet learnt how to harness the power you possess. You have not been taught how. It is unfortunate that school teaches you what to learn but never how to learn. And the best way you can unlock the superpowers your brain possess is to upgrade your brain by reading, just as you are now.

What intrigues you most about the human brain? Have you ever read a book, watched a movie or heard a story about a person who could achieve superhuman things with their brains? What was it? Your brain, when well trained can possess superhuman-like powers too!

_____

_____

_____

_____

_____

_____

_____

_____

_____

_____

_____

_____

_____

_____

_____

_____

_____

CHAPTER FOUR

HOW TO REMEMBER THIS (AND ANY) BOOK

Have you ever read something only to forget it the next day? Think back to that experience in high school or college. How did that feel? Write.

_____

_____

_____

_____

_____

_____

Your experience may have been because you approached reading, understanding and remembering the absolutely wrong way.

Research indicates that attention on a specific task usually wanes between 10-40 minutes. Therefore, a productivity hack is to use the Promodoro technique when you read or do any other thing that requires your active cognitive investment.

Break up the time you dedicate to reading into chunks of 25 minutes and 5-minute breaks. This is based on the principle of primacy and recency, which is to the effect that you are most likely to remember information you encounter at the beginning of your study sessions and the end. By creating several beginnings and endings, you dramatically improve the amount of information you can recall from your study sessions.

The second technique is to use what Jim Kwik calls the **F.A.S.T.E.R** method.

Forget

To learn effectively and develop a laser focus on the new material you are learning, you must forget three things.
The **first** is to forget what you think you already know about the topic. Push it out of your mind and develop a beginner's mentality towards the subject because preconceived notions about a topic may hinder you from learning the new.

The second key is to forget what's not important to your studies or what may distract you. For instance, put away your smartphone whenever you sit to read. Contrary to popular belief, your brain doesn't multi-task. Failure to be fully present will negatively affect your ability to comprehend and properly encode information.
Forget what is not urgent or important.

The third thing you must forget is your limitations, that is, the negative preconceptions you have about yourself that your memory is no good or you easily forget information after a short while no matter how hard you try.

What three things must you forget to make your study sessions more rewarding? What things distract you during your study sessions? Itemize them and make a conscious note to "forget" them in subsequent study sessions.

_____

_____

_____

_____

_____

_____

_____

_____

_____

_____

Act

Learning is not a passive experience; it is much more effective when you make it an active experience. So take your time and do all the exercises outlined in this workbook and take notes when you feel the need to. But don't make everything important and noteworthy.

State

Your state of mind and emotional disposition when you're learning new information greatly impact your ability to understand, properly encode and recall the information. If your most dominant emotion is boredom and lack of interest, you'll always forget.

Get excited about the new knowledge you are about to learn and how it will benefit you immensely. That way, you'll learn better.

What is your dominant emotion now? How energized, focused and motivated are you right now? Rate yourself, 0 is poor, and 5 is excellent.

What gets you excited and ready to learn? Write down one thing you'll always do to improve your state whenever you want learn new information.

_____

_____

_____

_____

_____

Teach

You assimilate information better when you teach it to other people. If you want to shorten your learning curve dramatically, learn this and every other material and teach it to other people. What's more, you get to learn when reading and a second time when teaching.

Enter

Most people enter everything on their calendars but forget to schedule a time for personal development. If it's not on your calendar, then it's most likely not going to be done.

Analyze your daily schedule and enter a time for your personal development for each day. You may use this time to read a book, learn a skill, or do any other productive thing.

DAY	PRODUCTIVITY TIME
Sunday	
Monday	
Tuesday	
Wednesday	

Thursday	
Friday	
Saturday	

Review

Always take a moment to recall and review the information you learned in your last reading session before you continue your next session. Practicing active recall and reviewing learned information has been shown to increase recall ability and strengthen knowledge dramatically.

Finally, you must **prepare your mind.**

To prepare your mind, you must continually ask yourself questions about the information you acquire. Whenever you get new information that particularly tellingly strikes you (information from this workbook inclusive), ask yourself:

- How can I use this?
- Why must I use this?
- When can I use this?

Asking and answering these questions about new information will help you assimilate better and make it long-term.

The work-section below will help you achieve that. You can make copies of it and work through the magic questions for new information you will learn as you read through this workbook.

NEW INFO LEARNED	
HOW CAN I USE IT?	
WHY MUST I USE IT?	
WHEN CAN I USE IT?	

NEW INFO LEARNED	
HOW CAN I USE IT?	
WHY MUST I USE IT?	
WHEN CAN I USE IT?	

PART II

LIMITLESS MINDSET: The What

"Before we address how to learn, we must first address the underlying beliefs we hold about what is possible."

The Mindset is made up of the assumptions, beliefs, and attitudes we hold about ourselves and the world surrounding us. It is the first part of the three-part Limitless Model.

Your mindset is what determines your response to and interpretations of your world.

However, we are not born with pre-installed mindsets about what we are capable of. Rather, it is a set of beliefs that we pick up from our childhood and our environment's totality as we grow from childhood to adulthood.

Limiting beliefs are thus, cultivated from childhood and establish firm roots as one grows into an adult.

Now is the time to unlimit yourself and get on the path to becoming Limitless!

CHAPTER FIVE

THE SPELL OF BELIEF SYSTEMS

Superheroes don't become superheroes by giving in to limiting beliefs. Regardless of their damaging history, moral conflict, and the darkness of their past, they go into every situation ready to save the day.

You are a superhero, and to realize your powers, you must begin with your belief systems, your mindset.

Until the 1950s, the belief was a human could not run a mile in less than 4 minutes. It was believed that the amount of effort required to break that barrier would cause the human body to break down, and no one did break that barrier until the 6th of May, 1954, when Roger Bannister ran a mile in 3 minutes and 59.4 seconds. Surprisingly, one month later, another athlete broke Bannister's record, and more than 1,400 athletes have achieved that feat since then.

The power of limiting beliefs kept athletes back from achieving that feat, and once it was shown that it was possible, more and more athletes became unlimited in that regard.

Limiting beliefs are often revealed in your self-talk, in what you are internally convinced you can never achieve.

Have you ever stopped yourself from doing something which you could ordinarily succeed at because you were convinced that it wasn't within your grasp or that you didn't have it within you to succeed?
Think long and hard and take some time to write down one of such experiences.

_____

_____

_____

_____

_____

_____

_____

_____

_____

That! Right there are limiting beliefs at work.

And if you extend that to other areas of your life, like your career options and ability to make friends, you'll discover that if your limiting beliefs are in control, you will wallow in underachievement, convinced that you don't deserve it.

You must come face-to-face with the voice in your head that judges you, doubts you, belittles you, and constantly tells you that you are not good enough. It says negative, hurtful things to you —"*I am such an idiot; I never do anything right; I will never succeed.*"

So, how do you minimize your limiting beliefs and develop a limitless mindset?

Jim Kwik proposes three keys:

Key one: Name your limiting beliefs

Some limiting beliefs have been explored in this workbook. For Jim Kwik, he believed he was the boy with the broken brain, and he could never read and understand.

Your limiting beliefs may have to do with your talent, your character, your relationships –things that are otherwise not related to learning at all.

Start paying attention to every time the belief wells up within you that you are incapable of a particular task. It might even seem to be an inconsequential area of your life, like the ability to tell jokes or sing. But the danger lies in the fact that negative self-talk affects how you think about your life in general.

So, think hard and list out what you've convinced yourself you are not good at or cannot do.

_____

_____

_____

_____

_____

_____

_____

_____

Knowing how you are holding yourself back with negative self-talk is extremely liberating because you get to see just how you are limiting yourself. More importantly, you'll realize that these are not really facts about who you really are. They are merely opinions that don't deserve the credence you give them.

Key Two: Get to the Facts

Sadly, some of the most dominant limiting beliefs that hold us back are so plain wrong in most cases. Are you *really* the dumbest person you know? Do you *really* terribly suck at holding conversations with people? Are you *really* incapable of remembering anything you read? What's the evidence to support all these self-limiting assumptions?

Most times, because your limiting beliefs are so connected to you emotionally, you fail to examine facts and opt to feel really terrible based on your negative self-talk.

Now, take one or two of your limiting beliefs you identified in number one and examine them below. Consider whether, in reality, there is any evidence to prove that you are hampered in that area and how much of that "evidence" is exaggerated by the voices in your head. Do you give yourself less credit than you deserve in that area? Get to the facts.

_____

_____

_____

_____

_____

_____

_____

_____

_____

_____

Key Three: Create New Beliefs

In the second Key, you examined various instances and got to the facts of your limiting beliefs. You may have found that you don't suck so much at speaking in public, or you're not that much of a complete failure when it comes to creating and maintaining relationships or reading and remembering facts.

Now that you have identified your limiting beliefs and examined their truth, the next step is to create new beliefs to replace your years of negative self-talk. These new beliefs will be truer than the lies you have been accepting about the reality of who you are and more beneficial to the limitless you that you want to create.

In the exercise that follows, you will write down your limiting beliefs you identified in Key one on the one hand and write down the new beliefs you have created for them on the other. These new beliefs will be truer than the lies you have been accepting about the reality of who you are and more beneficial to the limitless you that you are creating.

For instance, if your old belief was that you are a failure, your new will be that no one triumphs 100% all the time, but you are proud of yourself for how many times you perform at your best when pressure is highest, for the many times you made a friend or two laugh their bowels out though you are not much of a joke-teller, for the times you could focus and read so much in a short while.

These new beliefs will take out your self-limiting beliefs and give you a healthier mindset primed for success when the next situation comes along.

So, turn the page, get to work and create your new beliefs.

OLD BELIEF I HAD ABOUT MYSELF	NEW BELIEF I AM CREATING
❶	
❷	
❸	

OLD BELIEF I HAD ABOUT MYSELF	NEW BELIEF I AM CREATING
4	
_____	_____
_____	_____
_____	_____
_____	_____
_____	_____
_____	_____
_____	_____
5	
_____	_____
_____	_____
_____	_____
_____	_____
_____	_____
_____	_____
_____	_____
6	
_____	_____
_____	_____
_____	_____
_____	_____
_____	_____
_____	_____
_____	_____

CHAPTER SIX

THE SEVEN LIES OF LEARNING

LIES are Limited Ideas we Entertain. More so, we are being fed these lies so often we tend to believe them. That is dangerous because these lies are the antithesis to our quest to become limitless, learn faster and unlock our exceptional lives.

Jim Kwik exposes seven of these Limited Ideas Entertained:

INTELLIGENCE IS FIXED

Every one of us has the potential for genius. We choose to believe we are geniuses or not, or we are talented or not, because it relieves us of the responsibility to take charge of our lives.

Intelligence is never fixed; you have an infinite potential for growth if you can cultivate a growth mindset because a fixed mindset holds people back. That's why you must watch your attitude and language because that's where a fixed mindset manifests itself. If you catch yourself saying, "I am not good at learning," the statement implies that you believe that's a fixed situation and nothing you can do will improve the situation. Rather, say, "this is not something I am good at, *yet*."

Intelligence is fluid and ever-growing, depending on your mindset.

What do you think about your intelligence? Do you believe it's something you can improve? Why or Why not?

_____

_____

_____

_____

_____

WE ONLY USE 10% OF OUR BRAINS

The myth that we are using only 10% of our brain capacity at a given time has spread through history. Books, movies, and even scientific sources have been responsible for promoting this myth. But it remains what it is, a myth.

Jim Kwik believes that we actually have a 100% capacity of our brain capacity available to us. Like our physical bodies, some people only train themselves to make more use of their brains than others.

What you need to do is learn the most efficient and effective ways to harness the power of your brain.

MISTAKES ARE FAILURES

Albert Einstein is one of the most popular scientists of our modern era.

Yet Albert Einstein made mistakes –a lot of them. His development was even considered as slow, and he wasn't even the brightest of students. But Einstein is synonymous today with scientific genius and not mistakes.

So why are we so afraid of making mistakes?

Mistakes are not failures; they're only an opportunity to learn the correct thing. Moreover, you make mistakes, and mistakes don't make you; hence it is not how we make mistakes but how we deal with them that defines us.

You may have made some mistakes in the past. Have you let these mistakes define you or your approach to that activity in any way? How has your mindset changed now that you know it's a Limited Idea you Entertained?

_____

_____

_____

_____

_____

_____

_____

_____

_____

KNOWLEDGE IS POWER

Surprising, right?

The mere possession of knowledge is not going to help you. It is actually what you do with the knowledge you possess that matters. Knowledge is not power; it only has the potential to be. And until you read and apply the new knowledge you acquire in practical areas of your life, you have acquired no power.

Power is the application of knowledge, not knowledge in itself.

LEARNING NEW THINGS IS DIFFICULT

Learning new things *may* be difficult, but in the end, it is your attitude to learning that matters.

The key is to approach learning methodically, taking small, simple steps like the stonecutter who hammers away at a big stone for what seems like an eternity until it comes apart all of a sudden.

Approach learning like a stonecutter –patient and adaptive to your own needs, knowing that learning is not hard; what is more accurate is understanding that learning is a process, a set of methods that you can make easier for you if you learn how to learn.

Have you ever learned what is conventionally considered difficult? How did that change your approach to the subject? If you can't think of any "difficult" activity you learned, think of one now and resolve to learn it. It may be a new language or an activity like playing the guitar.

_____

_____

_____

_____

_____

_____

_____

_____

THE CRITICISM OF OTHER PEOPLE MATTERS

The biggest travesty in the world is people limiting and preventing themselves from expressing who they really are because of what others may think.

Children are always ready to learn and do indeed learn so much because they have no fear of what others may think of them. They just do!

To become limitless, you must let go of the fear of criticism from others that so cripples you. It just doesn't matter.

Creating the life you want is scary, but what's even scarier is regret. People will always doubt and criticize you, but that shouldn't faze you because when your life's journey is over, all that'll matter is how much you achieved and not how much people criticized you.

How do you handle criticism? Will anything change now that you know other's criticisms of you don't really matter?

_____

_____

_____

_____

_____

_____

GENIUS IS BORN

Genius is never born. It is made through deep and persistent practice —a perfect example of this the famed philosopher and martial arts legend Bruce Lee.

Bruce Lee was not quite the child that had the potential or could be seen as genius. His family had to move from San Francisco to Hong Kong while he was still a boy, and a short while later, Hong Kong was occupied by Japan. This set up a challenging social and political environment for a boy who was neither fully Chinese like his peers nor fully American like the other kids in his private school.

When Bruce was 13, he was taken in by a famous martial arts teacher to learn a special style of Kung Fu. Yet, he had to constantly fight the other kids in the class to prove himself and his abilities until his fighting spilled to the streets.

Fed up with his fighting antics, his father gave him a $100 bill and asked Lee to go back to America. But Lee would not. Instead, he washed dishes and did menial jobs to survive.

Later, Lee started teaching martial arts, and that's where his genius shone through. His methods were unlike any fighting method because he considered fighting the ultimate medium of self-expression.

Lee's talent was born due to a confluence of bad experiences and tensions he experienced as a kid.

But would you look at a kid with a propensity for street fights and poor grades at school and ever predict that he will become a master philosopher and teacher? No, you sure would not.

Genius is not born; it is made.

Did you believe any of these LIEs as true? Which of them and how did the LIE affect your mindset?

_____

_____

_____

_____

_____

Can you think of other LIE apart from these 7? Think long and hard, write them down and explain it in the clearest way possible.

_____

_____

PART III

LIMITLESS MOTIVATION: THE WHY

"Motivation is not something you have, it's something you do"

Motivation is the purpose one has for taking a particular action. It is the energy required to perform a set of tasks at any given time. Contrary to popularly held belief, motivation, like your mindset, is not fixed. It's something that continues to change every day. You could have the motivation to do both productive and non-productive things.

Motivation is the sum of purpose, energy, and small, simple steps.

You need a clear sense of purpose on what you want to do and what you hope to gain from it; it is what drives you to act. Secondly, you must generate sufficient energy to keep you active, and finally, using small, simple steps requires minimal effort and will keep you from being overwhelmed.

According to Jim Kwik, that is the surefire recipe to motivation, and this section is about teaching you how to have unshakeable motivation towards learning and life in general.

How do you understand about motivation? How does it occur according to Jim Kwik?

_____

_____

_____

_____

_____

_____

_____

_____

CHAPTER SEVEN

PURPOSE

Jim Kwik's lifelong weakness is lack of sleep. Since he was the kid with the broken brain, he had to work thrice as much as everyone else, even to make a semblance of coming close to them in his class performance. He could do this because he had the ultimate purpose of working hard to make his family proud. Hence his purpose was pretty clear; he had great motivation.

But even as he grew up, learned how to learn, and became incredibly good at learning, Kwik continued to work extremely hard. The reason why he continued to work so hard to make speech after speech, podcast after podcast, even while he was sleep-deprived, exhausted, and extremely introverted, came back to his extreme sense of purpose –he doesn't want anyone to suffer the way he did. The mission that drives him is to unlock brighter and better brains.

To get a clear picture of your purpose and drive, you must **start with why**. You must convey to yourself and others *why you do what you do*. "Why" is what drives your actions.

You hear the words purpose and goals every day. But do you know how they're different? A goal is a point you want to achieve, and purpose is **why** you want to achieve a goal.

Part of the answer to creating a sustainable sense of purpose is making SMART goals. Whether your goal is to read one book a week, get in shape, or start eating healthy, they must be SMART.

- **S is for specific**: Create specific goals. Don't say you want to get in shape; say you want to lose 20 pounds in the next 30 days.

- **M is for Measurable:** If you can't measure your goal, there's no way you can manage it. Don't say you want to get rich; decide you want to make $300,000 yearly for the rest of your life.

- **A is for Actionable:** You must develop action steps to achieve your goals.

- **R is for Realistic:** If you set unrealistic goals, you're more likely to give up on them before you start pursuing them.

- **T is for Time-based:** Give yourself a time-frame within which to achieve your goals.

In the exercise that follows, enter your SMART goals in the left column and state your purpose on the right.

GOAL I WANT TO HAVE MOTIVATION FOR	WHY I WANT TO DO IT (MY PURPOSE)
❶	
❷	
❸	
❹	

YOUR IDENTITY AND MOTIVATION

More often than not, what's not discussed in the quest for motivation is identity but the underlying perception of who you think you are plays a big part in motivating you or otherwise.

For instance, if your goal is to quit smoking, and you keep identifying yourself as a smoker by saying "I am a smoker," then it'll become extremely hard for you to quit.

You experience enormous power when you consciously associate or dissociate yourself with the goal you have.

If you've been telling yourself that your brain is sh*t and you can't learn anything, then you need to start telling yourself that you're a fast and efficient learner because the highest human drive is to act consistently with what it thinks it is.

Here and now, write down five "I am" statements consistent with whom and what you want to be:

1. I am _____

2. I am _____

3. I am _____

4. I am _____

5. I am _____

MOTIVATED BY LOSS OR REWARD

Motivation is a set of pleasurable or painful emotions that fuel your actions. It comes from connecting with your purpose and fully feeling the consequences of your actions or inactions –which may be reward on the one hand, or loss on the other.

Here's a simple exercise you need to do to fully understand how to be motivated through the rewards of your actions or loss occasioned by your inaction:

Outline your goals and think about the disadvantages you will suffer if you fail to perform the activity you want to get motivated to do. For instance, you may say that "I will never get to learn how to learn and settle for mediocre results at school or my job," or "I will never realize my potential." Make sure you feel the emotion of your answers. On the other hand, think about the advantages you will enjoy if you learn and follow through with your goals. It may be something like "I can finally get to ace my tests, be a better public speaker, learn new languages with ease and travel the world." You get the point.

My Goal	Reward For Following it Through	Loss on Failure to do so
1.		
2.		

3.		
4.		
5.		

The simple psychology of this exercise is that these advantages and disadvantages of following up on your goals will constantly motivate you to take action. Apply it to every activity you engage in.

CHAPTER EIGHT

ENERGY

Even when you have a clear purpose for doing something and you're pumped and ready to execute, what may keep you from being motivated is fatigue.

You need excellent mental and physical vitality to provide the much needed fuel for your goals and actions. Jim Kwik recommends ten ways to keep yourself agile and guarantee limitless brain energy to keep you motivated.

1. A Good Brain Diet

Research has proven that there's a direct connection between what you eat and your brain's health, therefore you must feed your brain with the best foods possible.

Here are the top 10 brain foods to incorporate into your daily diet:

a) Avocados

b) Blueberries

c) Broccoli

d) Dark Chocolates

e) Eggs

f) Green Leafy Vegetables

g) Salmon, Sardines, and Caviar

h) Turmeric

i) Walnuts

j) Water

Which of these brain foods are your favorites? How will you include them in your everyday diet?

_____

_____

_____

_____

_____

_____

2. Brain Nutrients

Research shows that particular nutrients have direct positive results on our cognitive ability. So if for any reason you cannot get a regular brain-rich diet, then there are supplements that may be perfect for you.

However, it's a good idea to consult with your physician to see what nutrients you are deficient in before getting of any of them. You can combine these supplements (do your research about them) with the brain foods mentioned in the previous recommendation.

3. Exercise

Exercise is extremely valuable if you want to unshackle your brain and get it performing at optimal levels. Aerobic exercise, the kind that gets your heart and sweat glands pumping harder have been shown to increase the size of the hippocampus, the part of the brain responsible for verbal memory and learning. Do you already have an exercise schedule? If not, fill out the table below and stick to your commitment.

DAY	EXERCISE TIME
Monday	
Tuesday	
Wednesday	
Thursday	
Friday	

| Saturday | |
| Sunday | |

4. Kill ANTs

ANTs are "Automatic Negative Thoughts," and like most people, you might have been entertaining such thoughts like you just don't have the smarts in you to do anything or you're not attractive enough or some other negative self-talk. If you regularly tell yourself that you can't do something then you won't do it. Kill these self-debilitating ANTs and accomplish whatever it is you set your sights on!

What's your biggest ANT? Tell yourself it's not true and replace that with an APT (Automatic Positive Thought)

_____

_____

_____

_____

5. A Clean Environment

A clean environment goes beyond the quality of air. Removing cluster and distractions from your surroundings will leave you feeling much lighter and primed for learning.

What will you do today and always to make your environment clean and conducive for learning?

_____

_____

_____

6. A Positive Peer Group

It's a widely held belief that you are an average of the top five people you mingle with. Though the belief might have been proven empirically, it holds some semblance of truth as the company you keep obviously affects your self-talk and overall self image. Make sure to keep a positive peer group if you want to unlimit yourself.

7. Brain Protection

That supercomputer between your ears is one of the most priceless gifts on earth. Make sure you protect it and avoid activities that may lead to accidents and brain damage. Even if you like extreme sports and other risk-related activities, make sure you take adequate steps to protect yourself and brain from damage.

8. New Learning

As long as you keep learning, you create new pathways in your brain. Learning is therefore one of the top activities you can engage in to keep your brain at optimal performance levels.

What new things would you like to learn?

_____

_____

_____

_____

9. Stress Management

Our bodies deal with stress by releasing a hormone known as cortisol into the body to counteract the physical rigors associated with stress. This in itself is not bad but the constant release of this hormone causes it to be accumulated in the body and the effect is inimical to optimal brain performance. With stress proven to be harmful to your brain, finding ways to relieve, or even avoid stress is paramount.

What do you do to ease stress? When was the last time you did it? Make a resolution to do it more often.

_____

_____

10.   Sleep

Good sleep is a must get if you want clearer focus and better memory. Lack of sleep makes concentration harder and prevents your brain from creating new pathways that are integral to learning and forming new memories.

Have you ever worked late into the night and gone to bed late? Do you notice how your brain is always fuzzy and your feeling generally hazy the next morning? Good sleep is not optional, it is a must have.

What are your sleeping habits? What can you do to improve your sleeping? For instance, you may decide to forgo the use of your devices at night before bed.

_____

_____

CHAPTER 9

SMALL SIMPLE STEPS

You now have a clear sense of purpose and the energy required to carry out your tasks and goals. Then what?

To accomplish your goals, you need to consistently make tiny or simple efforts everyday that require minimal energy but lead you to your goals over time. It is basically creating a habit of consistent, simple efforts.

We consistently struggle to act even when we have a clear sense of purpose and consistent motivation because we feel overwhelmed by the things we need to do. This is because, most times, we look at a project or goal in its entirety and get overwhelmed by the sheer size of the task at hand.

It is proven that unfinished tasks create tension in your brain, so do not beat yourself up for not getting around to doing the stuff you want to do, rather you should break down your goals or projects into small, simple tasks that you carry out every day, which not only get you closer to completing the project over time but also become your habits.

What you need to do is take what Jim calls "baby steps" towards the accomplishment of your goals. You're overwhelmed by the amount of material you need to study for your certification exam? Set a goal for yourself of reading just a few pages every morning. You can't get yourself to write the speech you need to make at next month's conference? Why not write the keynote to the speech now?

By breaking down tasks into smaller, simpler steps, the path to accomplishing them become clearer.

Think about a goal or task that you've been putting off for a while now. What is it? Break it down into bits that you can start performing today.

_____

_____

_____

_____

_____

_____

Small Simple Steps and Habit

There's a catch in all of these. Repeated small, simple steps become habits and habits are the very foundations of who and what we are. A habit is a solution to the recurring problems that you encounter all through your life, a solution that you have employed so many times that you don't even need to think of it.

For each habit that you have, it is motivated by the Habit Loop, what James Clear, author of the book *Atomic Habits* identifies as consisting of a **cue, a craving, a response,** and finally, **reward.** Let's look turning on the light in a room. The **cue** is walking into a room and finding it pitch dark, the **craving** is the feeling that you'll be more comfortable if the lights are on, the **response** is that you flip on the switch, and the **reward** is that the room is no longer dark.

You can apply this habit loop to any of your habits, even negative ones like eating too much. The cue here is walking close to or looking at your refrigerator, the craving is the knowledge that your cookies are in the refrigerator and your innate desire to eat them, the response is that you go over, open the fridge and take out the cookies, the reward is that you eat them and feel that crunchy, fatty sweetness all over again.

Can you identify some of the cues and responses for the bad habits you want to break to become limitless?

Bad Habit I want to break	Cue	Craving

So, because you want to become limitless, how do you break bad habits and form new small simple steps that'll help you achieve your goals?

For behavior change to occur there must be sufficient **motivation**, great **ability** and efficient **prompts**. Dr. B.J. Fogg, author of the book *Tiny Habits* calls explains these three prerequisites for behavior change in what he calls the Fogg Behavior Model.

Motivation may be pleasure or pain, hope or fear and social acceptance or rejection.

Fogg equates **ability** with simplicity. That is when something is really simple to do; we are more likely to carry it out. Let's look at some classes of ability.

The first is **time,** we consider something simple if we have the time available to do it. The second is **money**, if something requires huge financial commitment, then we don't consider it simple. Third, is **physical effort** hence we consider things that require relatively small physical effort as simple.

The last requirement for behavior change is **prompts**. There are three of these according to Fogg's Behaviour Model. These include:

1. **A Spark:** This is a type of prompt that immediately leads to a form of motivation. For instance, if driving gives you a fear of what may happen on the road, you're likely to adopt a habit that will change that fear.

2. **Facilitator:** This prompt works when motivation is high but ability is low. For instance, if you really want to study Engineering but you don't have the required funds, a scholarship will make you more than likely to take up the studies.

3. **Signal:** A signal serves as a reminder for your goals when both motivation and ability is high. For instance, if you love making smoothies, all you need do is walk into your kitchen and see the blender to prompt you to make one.

Your New Small Simple Steps

Now that you understand, Fogg's behavior model and the fact that making new habits you consider good for yourself is to integral to accomplishing your goals and important for your growth. How do you make new habits? The answer is you **WIN**.

W is for Want: Make sure you really want it. It is almost impossible to make a habit out of something you don't want.

I is for Innate: Your new habit must resonate with your innate desires.

N is for Now: Create a prompt that reminds you to perform the habit. It might be creating a reminder on your phone or placing something at home or office that reminds you of your new habit.

New Habit to Become Limitless	Prompt I am creating for the Habit
1.	

2.	
3.	
4.	
5.	

CHAPTER TEN

FLOW

Flow is the experience of being so deeply immersed in what you do, that time stops and nothing else seems to matter. It is accompanied by effortlessness, absolute concentration, total focus on goals and a feeling of reward from the experience.

Flow gets you so engrossed in what you do that you have no idea that afternoon has become night. It tremendously boosts your productivity.

Have you ever been in a state of flow? What were you working on? How did it feel? What did you achieve at the end?

_____

_____

_____

_____

TO become limitless, you have to get yourself into the flow state as often as possible, so how do you find flow? There are five things you must do:

Eliminate Distractions: Put everything else aside and concentrate completely on the task at hand. Checking out a text or social media after every minute is not going to keep you in flow.

Give Yourself Enough Time: Make sure you have enough time to get into flow, ideally two hours.

Do Something You Love: Getting into flow has much to do with the task at hand. If you're doing something you really love doing, then getting into flow won't be hard.

Have Clear Goals: If you don't have a clear idea of what you want to accomplish, finding flow will be difficult, if not impossible. Have a clear mission for what you want to do and see yourself disappear into the productive bliss of flow.

FIGHTING THE ENEMIES OF FLOW

Flow has some super villains that you must continually fight. These are:

Multitasking: Being a great multitasker is not equal to being limitless. Don't multitask, it spreads your attention thin and prevents you from reaching flow consistently. Rather, clear your schedule of everything else and focus completely on the task at hand.

Stress: Stress is one among the "master super villains." Do you ever find yourself suddenly thinking about work, family or relationship issues when you are trying to work on a task? Make your space impenetrable by outside stressors so you can work without distraction on the task before you.

Fear of Failure: Don't try to be perfect. It will only hamper your ability to get into flow. To defeat the fear of failure, convince yourself that lack of perfection is not only very welcome but a clear sign that you are pushing yourself in the ways that you must.

Lack of Conviction: The absence of belief in your approach to the task at a hand is a villain that you must contend with to get into flow. This is because the brain picks up any faint trace of uncertainty and releases cortisol, a stress hormone which disrupts memory and attention.

Which of the enemies of flow combats you more in your daily life? Now that you have itemized it, how can you overcome it?

_____

_____

_____

_____

_____

_____

_____

PART IV

LIMITLESS METHODS: THE HOW
"Methods differentiate limitless people from those who are encumbered by their limitations."

A method refers to the procedure for accomplishing something. In this instance, it is the procedure of learning how to learn, also known as Meta-learning.

This part is all about dismantling the ineffective ways of learning that you have been thought in school and teaching you the methods Jim Kwik used to transform himself from being the boy with the broken brain to a renowned authority in brain fitness and learning.

CHAPTER ELEVEN

FOCUS

Focus allows us to train our brain power fixedly on a particular task and burn through it with ease just as much as a magnifying glass focuses the rays of the sun on a dry leaf to burn through it. When we fail to focus our attention, we are hardly able to get through tasks because we not committed enough – emotionally and physically –to seeing such a task through. Focus' main villain is distraction.

How to Train Your Focus

Practicing focus requires constant practice and awareness. It is the ability to train your concentration on a particular task for extended periods. If you're working on a task and you feel your attention drifting to other things, consciously note what's happening to yourself and deliberately use your willpower to bring back that glowing light of concentration to the task at hand.

Furthermore, always try to avoid multitasking (which has already been explained. Don't scroll through social media if you are on the phone and don't work on your to-do list if you're preparing breakfast). Clear your working space of clutter may compete for your attention.

Another key to training your focus is to clear your busy mind.

Almost every moment of every day, we are being bombarded with stimuli on so many levels that disrupt our thought flow and give rise to anxiety. How can you get to be calm and clear your mind despite all these?

There are three things you can do even if you have few minutes:

Breathe: Deep cleansing breathes are so valuable in helping you re-center yourself. Here's how. Exhale completely through your mouth, close your mouth and inhale slowly and quietly to a mental count of four. Hold your breath to a count of seven and exhale slowly again. Repeat the cycle four times.

Do What's Causing you Stress: If you're finding it extremely difficult to focus, then it is very probable that there's something you need to do that you've been avoiding. Go get it done and come back with increased focus for the task at hand.

Schedule Your Distraction Time: If you get distracted a lot, just saying "I'll worry about that later" will not keep the distracting thoughts at bay. However, if you say, "I'll attend to that by 6:00pm, you're more likely to focus on the task at hand. Spell out your distraction time in your schedule.

What do you usually do to remain focused on tasks you work on? Have they been effective? How can the methods suggested by Jim Kwik change things for you?

_____

_____

_____

_____

_____

_____

_____

_____

_____

CHAPTER TWELVE

STUDY

You can learn how to unlimit your studies and when you finally do, it'll be a skill that you'll employ for the rest of your life. Most people do not know how to study effectively because they have not been taught. But you need to move to the level of unconscious competence as far as your study is concerned in order to be limitless.

Here are some habit tips from Jim to unlimit your studies:

Employ Active Recall: Active recall is the process of mentally reviewing a material and immediately checking to see how much of it you remember. Forcing yourself to recall is one of the most effective methods to truly learn any material. To employ active recall, read or view the material you are learning then close the book or pause the video. Now try writing down all that you remember from the material. Do this a few times over concentrating on the areas you failed to remember in the last recall process and see your study sessions become more productive.

Spaced Repetition: Space out reviews of your material over days (maybe once every day) and focus more heavily on the parts you can't remember.

Manage the State You're in: Your emotional state determines how effective your study sessions turn out to a large extent. Always get yourself pumped and excited for studies and sit straight during studies as your posture affects your mood.

Music for the Mind: Music has been proven to aid learning. Jim Kwik recommends you play some baroque music in the background while studying.

Listen with your Whole Brain: Listening is integral to learning but we often fail to learn well because we don't apply our whole brain power to the listening exercise. Use **HEAR** to listen with your whole brain. **H**alt other activities and concentrate fully, get into the speaker's emotional state with **E**mpathy. Develop enthusiasm by **A**nticipating what the speaker has to say and finally **R**eview what you have learnt by asking questions to gain clarity or reviewing it to yourself.

Have you ever used any of the methods suggested by Jim Kwik to study? Did they work for you? Which ones are new? Resolve to use them henceforth.

CHAPTER THIRTEEN

MEMORY

There can be no learning without memory. This chapter teaches you the basic principles of memory. However, the most basic of these is **MOM**.

Motivation: Would you remember that you're to visit a friend on the 22nd of June 2022 if he promised he's going to give you $100,000 when you do? Of course you will. You are more likely to remember when you attach value to whatever you learn. In other words, the memory works best when there's some form of motivation for the learning activity.

Observation: You fail to remember because you don't pay *attention* to the learnt information which may be a person's name or anything at all. Condition yourself to be in the *present* in any situation you want to remember something.

Methods: The methods you can use to have a better memory are discussed below. Make sure you always carry them in your mental toolkit.

To get the best returns on your learning, make sure you approach it as an active rather than passive activity.

Here are some memory tools t tremendously increase your memory.

Visualization: Your visual memory is very powerful and that's why you think in pictures. Always try to see the pictures or imagery of what you're trying to learn depicts rather than the words themselves and see your memory skyrocket!

Association: Association is the key to all learning. It means connecting new learnt information to that which you already know. Do you have special memories? Like a song that reminds you of another person? A smell that reminds you of a place? Make conscious connections between these special memories and new learnt information to retain and remember better.

Emotion: You're likely to remember learnt information if you make it humorous, adventurous or action filled. Attach emotion to learnt information and see your ability to remember skyrocket!

The Method of Loci: Locations

The method of loci is a great tool you can use to dramatically increase your memory. It is associating information with specific locations which may be a familiar street or your room, just any place familiar. The goal is to break down the information you want to learn into bits and associate each bit with chosen spots in your preferred location. For instance, if you walk through your room, there's the lamp in the corner, then your bed, then the door to the restroom etc. Associate each bit of the learnt information to these places and as you mentally walk through the chosen location, you are able to recall all the information associated with those places.

Let's try this Instructive Exercise.

Imagine that you want to remember the following words in the order which they appear.

Love, Joy, Peace, Patience, Kindness, Goodness, Faithfulness, Self-control, and Gentleness.

For the untrained memory, a person may start calling the words over and over again to encode it in the memory which is never ever effective.

What we'll do is embark on a journey through "places" or "locations" we are already familiar with. A good place to always use is your house.

So for this exercise, we'll use three rooms and nine locations to remind us of the nine items:

Room 1 the TV Room: 1. Couch 2. Table 3. The TV

Room 2 the Kitchen: 4. Fridge 5. Stove 6. Oven

Room 3 the Bedroom: 7. Bed 8. Mirror 9. Window

What you have to do is turn all the items into something tangible and associate them to the places such that each location automatically reminds you of the equivalent item.

Let's start with the TV Room. The first word is **Love**. Imagine a couple playing on your couch. What's the relationship between them? **Love.**

At the **Table**, imagine jumping for **joy** when you find an appointment letter for a job you applied lying there.

At the TV Room, you're watching a movie and a husband kisses his wife good morning. What does kiss remind you of? **Peace**.

At the **Fridge**, imagine you open it and find snails inside. What comes to mind when you see a snail? Slow, **patience**.

Imagine you cook a delicious meal on the stove and offer it to a homeless man standing beside the stove. This reminds you about being kind, **kindness.**

The next item we want to remember is goodness. Imagine jam floating in the oven; Jam is food. Food sounds like good. So you have your next word, **goodness**.

In the bedroom, the bed reminds you of a married couple. They are supposed to be **faithful** to each other.

The mirror lets you see your self. **Self-control.**

Finally, imagine a boy pushing his brother off a window. That is rough. The opposite of rough is what? Gentle. **Gentleness**.

Now, what was the connection to each place? Try to remember and write it down without checking back the last page.

Couch	
Table	
TV	
Fridge	
Stove	
Oven	
Bed	
Mirror	
Window	

How did you do? You must have remembered most if not all of the words. Even if you did not, once you go over the list a few times and connect the images properly, you'll never forget those words again!

However, you must develop your own "locations" using environments you're already familiar with. This will help you create more vivid journeys.

The good news is that you can use this method to remember any information at all; whether you are a student learning basic things or an advanced algebraic mathematician, the potentials are limitless.

Exercise

Use locations you are already familiar with and encode the following words using imagery as has been done above.

Above, house, profits, knife, technology, average, sustainable, fan, and venue.

A Powerful Tip

The technique shown above can be used to remember almost anything and even to deliver stellar speeches without notes and do so brilliantly! Yes you read that right. Here's how:

First of all, write out your entire speech including all the important ideas and talking points. Read everything you've written to get a fair idea of what you're supposed to say.

Next, develop bullet points representing entire thoughts and reduce those points to keywords that will remind you of what you have to say as regards those points.

You're going to develop images for those key points and associate them to something you're already familiar with to enable you remember the keywords and thus the entire thought associated with it.

Let's imagine you're giving a speech to some local businessmen on how to increase their business profits. Your keywords may be the ones shown below:

Increasing profits, communication, time management, Goals, Reward, Teamwork, Hard work, Organization, Education, and Advertising.

For **Increasing Profits**, you can imagine loads of cash falling from the sky and filling up a parking lot. This would set up a cue to remind you of **increasing profits**.

For **communication,** you can link the first keyword to the second by imagining the dollar bills talking to the cars in the lot –**communication.**

Time management –A wall clock in the lot joins in on the conversation between the bills and the cars. Clock reminds you of **time management.**

You can then imagine that the bills, cars and the clock agree to football match which must produce **goals.**

Create mental images for the remaining words and see what you can come up with.

This technique is infinitely helpful even when studying academic materials. This is because you can reduce the whole material into main points which you finally turn into keywords. Then you create mental images for these keywords as already shown. This way, you will find learning faster and more efficient. The possibilities are indeed limitless with some bit of practice.

Remembering Names

Are you familiar with that frustration you feel when you can't recall the name of a person you met the last week when you two meet on the walkway again? To remember names you have to **BE SUAVE**.

Believe you can actually remember the name of anyone you meet. This is a fundamental first step.

Exercise by practicing what you are going to learn about remembering names now.

Say the name back to the person once they tell you. This will not only consolidate the name in your memory but also give you the opportunity to be sure that you heard right.

Use the name during your conversation with the person, for instance, "That's interesting Haldane," instead of "that's interesting."

Ask about the origin of the name if it's a less common and difficult name like "Ushahemba."

Visualize the name. This is a very effective memory tool. For instance, you can visualize a giant checkmark on their forehead if the person is Mark. This will help you remember when next you meet.

End your conversation by saying the person's name. For instance "Thanks Ushahemba, its been a real pleasure talking to you."

CHAPTER FOURTEEN

SPEED READING

Reading is a great activity that's necessary for learning. Leaders are readers and the importance of reading cannot be overemphasized. In fact, there's so much reading can do for you, like increasing your vocabulary, sharpening your focus, improving your memory, and helping your brain perform better.

However, before you learn how you can read faster, there are some misconceptions about speed reading that you must kill within you. These popular misconceptions which are entirely not true are that it's hard to read fast, faster readers can't comprehend well or properly appreciate reading. Entirely false!

So, how can you get to read faster?

1. Speed Reading Exercise

Get a book of your choice and set a timer for 4 minutes. Now read as you normally would until the timer counts down and mark out the place you stopped reading (that's your finish line). Now, set your timer for 3 minutes and read up to the finish line (using your finger) within those three minutes.

Next, set the timer for 2 minutes and try to get to the finish line within those 2 minutes. Don't worry about comprehension, use your finger to trace the lines and have your eyes follow as fast as possible. Now, set the timer for 1 minute and repeat same.

Finally, set your timer for 2 minutes and start reading an entirely new area than the one you previously used for the exercise (with comprehension). When the two minutes are up, count the number of lines you read and multiply by the number of words per line, then divide by two. That's your new reading rate.

With constant practice every day, your reading speed will increase until reading large amount of text will become a blitz for you.

In the table below, record the reading rate you get after you have done the exercise and finally read within two minutes (with comprehension) as described above. If you're doing everything right, you will see your reading rate increase within five days:

	Reading Rate
Day 1	
Day 2	
Day 3	
Day 4	
Day 5	

2. Expand your Peripheral Vision

Your peripheral reading vision refers to the number of words that your eyes can see when you glance at the material you're studying. Try to always read a group of words together rather than subvocalizing each word.

3. Counting

To practice speed reading, count out loud 1, 2, 3... as you read. This will prevent you from subvocalizing each word, rather you'll see them as images and soon, reading will become like watching a movie.

CHAPTER FIFTEEN

THINKING

To make big accomplishments like becoming limitless, you must adopt a new approach to thinking.

In the first instance, you can use the Six Thinking Hats proposed by Dr. Edward De Bono to make your thinking much more productive. The idea is to progressively don these hats metaphorically as you move through the thinking process.

i. You put on a **white hat** in information gathering mode when you're gathering facts and details to address the issue at hand. Think of a lab coat to remember this.

ii. Don the **yellow hat** as you look at the positives or value inherent any problem you are facing. Think of a smiling sun to remember this hat.

iii. Put on the **black hat** to consider the consequences of failing to successfully address the problem. A judge's robe should help you remember this hat.

iv. Don the **red hat** to allow emotions come into play in your thinking process, express your fears and concerns, you may also allow intuition and speculation to come into the picture. Use a **big red heart** to remember this hat.

v.   Now is time to get creative. Put on the **green hat** to look at the problem **analytically**. What new ideas can you bring to the problem? How can you approach solving it in a way you haven't thought about before? Use the mental image of **green grass** to remember this hat.

vi. Finally get into **management** mode with the **blue hat.** Here, make sure you've gone through the other hats productively and you have a concise conclusion.

This guide to thinking is incredibly ingenious because it allows you strategically move through the thinking process and get back the best returns. **Make copies** of the **worksheet** below and work through the hats each time you want to think about a specific problem and come to an ingenious solution that will leave you feeling limitless!!

PROBLEM I WANT TO THINK ABOUT AND SOLVE	_____ _____ _____
THE WHITE HAT "What facts do i have about the problem at hand?"	_____ _____ _____ _____ _____
THE YELLOW HAT What are the positives that I stand to gain? What are the benefits?	_____ _____ _____ _____
THE BLACK HAT Difficulties and pitfalls of the problem? The consequences of failing to solve it.	_____ _____ _____ _____
THE RED HAT "What are my fears and concerns about the problem?"	_____ _____ _____ _____
THE GREEN HAT "What new ideas can I bring to solve the problem?"	_____ _____ _____ _____
THE BLUE HAT "Did I effectively go through all the hats? What is my decision?"	_____ _____ _____ _____

Furthermore, there are mental models that train your mind to think and cultivate sharper problem solving and decision making skills.

MENTAL MODELS TO AID CRITICAL THINKING AND DECISION MAKING

According to Jim Kwik, some of the best mental models to aid your creative decision making and thinking include:

DECISION MAKING: The 40/70 Rule

This rule states that you should never make a decision on the strength of less than 40% of the information you are likely to get or more than 70% of the total information available. This is because anything less than 40% and you're plainly guessing while anything greater than 70% means you're stalling over the decision.

PRODUCTIVITY: Create a Not-to-do List

A not-to-do list may seem counterintuitive but it will help you decide right from the onset what you're going to put aside. This will help you overcome the feeling of overwhelm and focus on the tasks that truly matter hence you already know with certainty what you don't have time for.

PROBLEM SOLVING: Study Your Errors

Studying your mistakes has the tremendous power of turning your worst moments into opportunities for growth and learning. It is a much needed skill for problem solving.

STRATEGIC THINKING: Second-Order-Thinking

Second-order thinking refers to the ability to think about the consequences of the consequences of your actions and inactions.

To tap into the power of second-order thinking, always ask yourself, "And then what?" Secondly, you have to think progressively through time. "What will be the consequences of my actions tomorrow, in the next five days, five years from now..."

Second order thinking greatly improves your ability to think strategically and see what may not be immediately apparent.

Another major component to strategic thinking is to **think exponentially.** Exponential thinking is the ability to see things from a different mindset, to approach problem solving from a whole new perspective that goes to the very roots of the problem. It is addressing the cause of a problem rather than attacking the problem itself.

Jim Kwik **recommends these four steps** when next you're **confronted with a problem** to fire up your **exponential thinking** ability.

Get to the Underlying Problem: Sometimes the underlying cause of a problem may not be readily apparent. Brainstorm to get to it.

Posit a New Approach: "What if" statements are the keys to opening new paradigms for any problems you face. For instance, you can ask yourself, "what if you no longer had to use most of your day chitchatting and checking social media?" What if questions open us up to a new realm of possibilities.

Read About It: Reading is always a great way to learn how to solve problems. Whenever faced with a problem, read up as much as you can about it. It will help you think exponentially by giving you a well-rounded view of the subject.

Extrapolate: After identifying the underlying problem, posing what-if questions and doing your research by reading, the next step is to take a well informed decision based on the model of exponential thinking.

About EasyGrowth Publishing

Do you have so much to do but no time? Busy schedules and deadlines creeping up on you? A thousand and one things to attend to, leaving you no time to read all the books you want to read? Worry no longer! EasyGrowth Publishing is a busy man's solution to the busy person's problem. We are a group of experienced writers committed to providing you detail-oriented, straight-to-the-point, and high quality workbooks for, and summaries of lifechanging books by the world's best authors. We sift through the fluff and help you strike gold with each page you turn so you can become golden in as little time as possible.

Made in the USA
Las Vegas, NV
20 November 2024

12196723R00066